PRODUCTIVITY HABITS

PROVEN TECHNIQUES TO INCREASE PERSONAL PRODUCTIVITY AND ACHIEVE GOALS

Robert Hensley

CONTENTS

INTRODUCTION 7

CHAPTER 1: WHAT IS TIME MANAGEMENT? 9
- CRITICAL ELEMENTS OF TIME MANAGEMENT 9
- DEVELOPING TIME MANAGEMENT SKILLS 10
  - *Identification of the components of a big task* 10
  - *Knowing when to take a rest and reward oneself* 10
  - *Honing a never say die spirit* 10
  - *Dealing with pressure* 10
  - *Observe patterns with your use of time* 10
  - *Routine development* 11
  - *Time logging* 11
  - *The Control Mindset* 11

CHAPTER 2: BENEFITS OF TIME MANAGEMENT 12
- GREATER PRODUCTIVITY 12
- INCREASED OUTPUT 12
- INCREASED ENERGY 12
- FREEDOM TO DO WHAT YOU WANT 13
- REDUCED EFFORT 13
- MINIMUM WASTED TIME 13
- INCREASED OPPORTUNITIES 13
- MORE FREE TIME 13
- IMPROVED DECISION-MAKING ABILITY 14
- REDUCED STRESS 14
- FOSTERS SELF-DISCIPLINE 14
- MORE PRODUCTIVITY AND SUCCESS 14
- ACCOMPLISH MORE WITH LESS EFFORT AND TIME 15
- INCREASED LEARNING OPPORTUNITIES 15
- ENHANCED FLEXIBILITY AND SPONTANEITY 15
- A HAPPY AND HEALTHY LIFE 15
- BETTER WORK QUALITY 15
- COMPLETE TASKS ON TIME 16

CHAPTER 3: EFFECTIVE TIME MANAGEMENT TOOLS 17

GOAL SETTING 17
CREATE TO-DO LISTS 17
MAKING A SCHEDULE AND STICKING TO IT 18
TIME BLOCKING 19
START THE DAY RIGHT 21
   Start early *21*
   Make your bed *22*
   Sit down and plan your activities for the day *22*
   Wake your mind with the right stimulation *22*
   Focus on how you start your workday *22*
COMING UP WITH METHODS TO MAKE YOUR CHORES EASIER 23
   Use Tools that Make the Job Easier *23*
   Learn Tricks to Getting Tasks Done from Others *23*
   Look for Ways to Cut Corners Without Cutting Quality ... *23*
   Take the Advice of Others and Try it *24*
ESTABLISHING YOUR DAILY ACTIVITIES 24
PRIORITIZATION 24
   Tackling the difficult tasks first *26*
   Tackling easy tasks first *26*
   Make a list of all the tasks your project involves *26*
   Assess these tasks according to gravity and value *26*
   Organize these tasks into categories *26*
   Determine which tasks to cut *27*
PREPARE YOUR PLANNING TOOLS 27
GET ORGANIZED 28
AVOID PROCRASTINATION 28
   There is only now *29*
   Once You Do It, You Will Be Ok *29*
   Think About the Repercussions *29*
   Do whatever it takes *29*
   Take Breaks *30*
DELEGATE TASKS OR ACTIVITIES 30
   Control your instincts to hard work *31*
   You Can Delegate Down and What You Can Delegate Up *31*
   Give Clear and Concise Instructions *31*

Build the Competence and Empower People for Down-Delegation *31*
    Delegation Means "Let Go" *32*
AVOID MULTITASKING 32
PLAN YOUR TIME 33
    Plan Your Day the Night Before *33*
    Do Not Get Overwhelmed *33*
    Wake up Early *33*
    Sleep Early *33*
SETTING DEADLINES 34
ELIMINATE DISTRACTIONS 34
    Train your brain to focus *35*
    Break down huge tasks *35*
    Track your time expenditure *35*
    Block all distracting websites and apps *35*
    Create a schedule *35*
MANAGE INTERRUPTIONS 36
    Work When You Need to Work *36*
    Minimize all of the Interruptions *36*
    Ask Other People *37*

CHAPTER 4: HOW TO SET BOUNDARIES AND LEARN TO SAY NO 38
CREATE A MANTRA 39
KEEP A JOURNAL 40
PRACTICE 40

CHAPTER 5: IMPROVE YOUR PRODUCTIVITY BY IDENTIFYING YOUR PERSONAL VALUES 41
THE PURPOSE AND MEANING OF YOUR LIFE 41
THE MOST IMPORTANT THINGS IN YOUR LIFE 42
BELIEVE THAT YOU ARE SPECIAL 42
PERFORM SELF-ANALYSIS 42
SOME APPS FOR PRODUCTIVITY 43
    Focus Booster *43*
    Rescue Time *43*
    Any-Do *43*
    Toggl *43*
    To Do Calendar Planners *43*

Remember the Milk *44*
Time Doctor *44*
Google Calendar *44*
Todoist *44*
Focus @ Will *44*
Atracker *45*
Evernote *45*
If This Then That (IFTT) *45*

CHAPTER 6: HOW TO MANAGE YOUR WORK ENVIRONMENT 46
GET RID OF PHYSICAL CLUTTER 46
DE-CLUTTERING YOUR MIND 48
STAYING MOTIVATED 48
  Reward a Good Job Done *49*
  Take a Quick Break *49*
WATCH OUT FOR TIME KILLERS 49
  Checking Emails *49*
  Watching TV *49*
  Commuting *50*
  SmartPhones *50*
  Friendly Chatting *50*
  Surfing the Net *50*
  Social Media Networks *51*

CHAPTER 7: MANAGING TIME SPENT WITH OTHER PEOPLE 52
ALWAYS HAVE A GOAL WHEN MEETING PEOPLE DURING WORK HOURS 52
SHARE INFORMATION RELEVANT TO THE MEETING IN ADVANCE 53
REDUCE CHANCES OF MISCOMMUNICATION 53
LEAD WHEN NO ONE WANTS TO 53

CHAPTER 8: HEALTH'S ROLE IN TIME MANAGEMENT 54
EATING RIGHT 54
EXERCISING 55
SLEEP 56

Fun Time and relaxation 56

CHAPTER 9: IDENTIFYING THINGS THAT WASTE YOUR TIME...58
Time Killers 58
Dealing with Time Wasters.......................................59
  List your time wasters 59
  Resist the urge to respond to distracting stimuli 60
  Remove social media apps 60
  Make your breaks boring 60
  Keep your environment tidy 60
  Prepare activities for waiting and commuting..........61

CHAPTER 10: MANAGING YOUR PRODUCTIVITY 62
Divide your day into quadrants.................................62
Divide each quadrant into 15-minute chunks 62
Manage your energy 63
Motivate yourself for work right before a new quadrant starts 63

CHAPTER 11: IMPROVING YOUR TIME MANAGEMENT HABITS 65
Identify the nature of your activities 65
Analyze and re-strategize 65
Look for positive changes and make them your habits 66
Aim for efficiency 66

CHAPTER 12: ENJOYING A MOTIVATED AND PRODUCTIVE LIFE 67

CONCLUSION 69

Introduction

Time Management is how you organized your time and how long you intend to spend on each task. Everyone encounters time management issues. There are too many tasks, and there is too little time. You can't help but feel stressed the majority of the time. It's as if you have no control over your life; you cannot even think of the things that you consider essential. Your work grows more and more demanding and you seem to have no time left for yourself.

This eBook will teach you the basics of time management. It explains how you can manage your time effectively and increase your productivity. You will get all the tips and tricks you need to effectively manage your time in this guide.

This book has been designed to give you the bare bones on which you can build a more efficient and effective way of living your life, one that is structured, organized and one in which you are proactive and make the most of every opportunity that comes your way.

The most productive people manage their time wisely. They can manage it exceptionally well, even when they face a lot of pressure and even when their schedule is super tight.

This book discusses the skills, techniques, and other essential methods involved in fundamental time management.

That way, you'll have plenty of opportunities to enjoy your life more, on top of the goals you have set for yourself for business, self-management, and life goals. There are so many benefits that you can be gained from exceptional time management practices, which will be explained throughout this book.

Throughout this book, you will understand that no matter what kind of job you do, time management is an essential aspect. Playing Games that will help you develop your skills on time management at your free time are also suggested.

This material will arm you with time management hacks. That means you will have tips that you can use to plan your time well. These tips may be easy to understand but don't be blinded by their simplicity just apply them in your daily life and you will not regret. This is the guide you need to achieve anything in life without further ado let's get started.

Chapter 1: What Is Time Management?

Time management is a person's ability to manage their time, just like any critical skill related to your career, it can decide whether you will succeed as a professional or not. Time is an irreplaceable resource that can help you achieve your dreams. Consider it as a crucial asset that you cannot hoard or recover. You need to spend time on everything you do and gain excellent rewards if you can accomplish many things within the time available to you.

Time management is important in our lives because it enhances productivity and and improves our health. When you plan your time you will achieve inner peace, improve your mental health and build strong relationships. People who fail to manage their time are often stressed, anxious, or depressed. You will achieve higher energy and be more productive if you plan your time.

Critical Elements of Time Management

- Desire – It is imperative that you have the desire to control your time and achieve an improvement in your productivity.
- Decisiveness – This characteristic plays a vital role in your success: you have to make a firm decision to practice your time management skills until they turn into habits.

- Determination – Becoming an effective time manager involves various challenges. When faced with temptations to forget about what you are trying to do and go back to your old ways. Without determination, your chances of acquiring the necessary time management skills are close to zero.
- Discipline – Experienced time managers consider this as the most essential characteristic. You must have enough discipline to treat time management as an enduring practice. You should be willing to pay the price, do what is right, and perform activities at the right time, regardless of whether or not it benefits you in the short-term.

Developing Time Management Skills

Identification of the components of a big task

It takes talent to identify the small parts that make up a big task. However, you can learn this with practice. By learning how to do so, you can take small but sure steps towards your goal. Also, the good thing is you can distribute the other pieces to people who are willing to help.

Knowing when to take a rest and reward oneself

Believe it or not, taking regular breaks and rewarding oneself can improve a person's performance. It also helps one achieve more and become more efficient.

Honing a never say die spirit

It will not be all laurels for you. Sometimes, you will face failures and frustrations. More often than not, you will have to deal with backlogs. However, take heart and learn to adopt a never say die attitude. This way, you learn to rise from your weaknesses and limitations.

Dealing with pressure

Have grace whenever you face a big task. Never bow down to pressure. See it as motivation instead of being a source of stress. From time to time, take a break and relax. Remember, pressure won't go away if you succumb to it. Deal with it well and see good things coming your way.

Observe patterns with your use of time

Identify your peak time and label it as your prime time. Also, take note of those periods when you feel most distracted. Assess the kinds of activities where you waste your time and keep track of which ones are recurring. Of course, do something about it.

Routine development

Developing a routine for your work proves to be genuinely beneficial. In line with that, you need to keep your workspace as clean and as organized as possible, too. Also, you need to make a standard schedule for each of your workdays. Write down the details in case there are adjustments.

Time logging

A time log helps you avoid putting your precious minutes and hours to waste. In the process what you need to do is, create a chart for the entire week (divided into days). The days will then be divided into intervals of half an hour. For the next seven days, you should make it a point to note everything that you will and need to do. After seven days, examine the time log closely to look for periods where you could have been more productive. Also, you will see where your consistent "prime time" is and schedule your next tasks according to your findings.

The Control Mindset

Proper time management also encompasses the management of your mood towards work. Most people with no control over their emotions, motivations, and moods usually end up neglecting their plans.

If you want to take charge of your time, you should focus only on the things that you can control. Even if you are in difficult situations, you should not allow your mind to start blaming others or your environment.

You should continue the control mindset as you proceed with the rest of the book. In this mindset, you always ask yourself how you can control the situation. By doing so, you always expect a certain level of competence from yourself.

You can only control the way you use your time if you can control your motivation. Motivation is the mental state, emotion, or thought that encourages us to move towards our goals. You need to be aware of your different mental states because they are essential factors that affect your ability to stick to your planned schedule.

Chapter 2: Benefits of Time Management

Here are significant reasons why effective time management is necessary for anyone aiming to accomplish goals and achieve success.

Greater Productivity

One of the most significant benefits you stand to derive from practicing effective time management is improved productivity.

When you efficiently complete tasks, you save more time; you can then use the saved time to complete other essential tasks. When you complete more work your output increases.

Increased Output

Productivity increases when your mind is free from stress and hence, free to focus on the tasks that need to be completed without distractions. You not only complete the tasks you have set out to do but also find time to do other things that until now you could not do because of lack of time.

Increased Energy

Recall how you feel when you complete a task that required your intensive intervention. The satisfaction that you enjoy at the end of a work well done and completed on time releases the endorphins that make you feel good about yourself and more energetic. You will ready to take on the next task.

Freedom to Do What You Want
With time management you will find enough time to complete your "work" and still have enough left to bond with your family on a daily basis, socialize with friends and colleagues, take up a hobby, read a book – and in general do things that you would have otherwise thought impossible for lack of time.

Reduced Effort
You will find that with time management, the effort you require seems lesser because your mind is calm and focused, and you can concentrate your full attention on your work schedule.

Minimum Wasted Time
An unorganized person will spend much of the time searching for things, redoing things, handling situations resulting from mistakes, and so on. With time management, you learn how to work in a focused manner and therefore, commit fewer mistakes (ordinarily resulting from stress from mismanagement of time). It also helps to eliminate the time you would otherwise waste when re-engaging in a task you interrupted.

Increased Opportunities
Clarity of mind helps you think more creatively and hence, find more opportunities to grow. An uncluttered mind is more likely to open to new ideas that a mind burdened with 1001 things on it.

More Free Time
Time management is very vital at work, at school, or home. At times, you may feel as if you have too many tasks to complete and not enough time. However, if you plan your

tasks, schedule them, and complete every task within a set time, you will not waste time wondering what to do.

Improved Decision-Making Ability

Sometimes, when you feel as if you are pressed for time even when you must make a decision, it is easy to make the wrong decision without adequately considering the different options. On the other hand, if you practice proper time management, because you have planned, you will feel a sense of calm, which will eliminate the pressure, which often emanates from feeling as if you do not have enough time. Without the presence of this pressure, you will make conscious choices and spend your time doing valuable and meaningful activities.

Reduced Stress

When you control your time, you avoid the stress which comes with personal problems or frictions with others because you will know how long it will take to complete an activity and the best approach to use to complete a task within its prescribed time and deadline. You will have set goals for your day, prioritized essential tasks or activities, and created a detailed guide showing how you intend to tackle every activity or task.

Fosters Self-Discipline

Because your time management plan will guide and motivate you when you feel like avoiding an activity that needs completion, you will effectively prevent procrastination. You will be conscious of your goals and rewards or benefits that come from attaining your goals; hence, you will feel the urge to complete each task within the set time without leaving any activity or task undone.

More Productivity and Success

It is possible to be productive but not successful. You can do one activity to perfection and produce the best results possible but leave other activities undone that would have led you to attain your goals. When this happens, you will fail to achieve your short and long-term goals.

Accomplish More with Less Effort and Time
When you create a schedule that guides the time you spend on any given task, the very nature of effective time management, you accomplish more with less effort and time.

Increased Learning Opportunities
Learning is a continuous process, the more you learn the more valuable you become. Learning opportunities are everywhere. If you plan, organize, and control your time, you will complete your daily goals and have extra time to take advantage of learning opportunities.

You can use those opportunities to research an issue you feel that you need to get more information on, attend part-time classes, and assist coworkers or course mates on projects you will learn new skills.

Enhanced Flexibility and Spontaneity
When you have good time management habits, you can squeeze in unexpected activities and spontaneously make changes to your schedule when the need arises. You will be able to respond to any "emergency" immediately and at any time without leaving important daily activities unattended because you will quickly reschedule your activities or squeeze in any important unplanned activity into your extra time.

A Happy and Healthy Life
When you manage your time, you eliminate the need to complain about not having enough time to complete your tasks and activities. You will enjoy your life because every second, minute, an hour of your day will be well accounted and be prepared. You will control your life and will have enough time to deal with everything that comes your way.

Better Work Quality
By freeing your schedule and having extra time, you focus on improving your output quality. You discover what you need to do to improve your work, which enhances the quality

of your work. Moreover, time management also requires delegation of authority to the right people as a way to free up your time and direct it to the most critical tasks.

Complete Tasks on Time

By practicing effective time management, you manage to get everything done on time.

When you complete tasks and work on time, you eliminate the worry of missed deadlines, which leads to fantastic career opportunities.

If you want to enjoy the benefits of managing your time well, you MUST start learning essential time management.

Chapter 3: Effective Time Management Tools

Goal Setting

Where you want to be 5 years from today? What about 15 years from today? What about post-retirement? Have you thought about it? Have you visualized yourself in different stages in the future?

Without a clear-cut life goal, you would not have a direction. Even more important, you would not know whether you are successful or not. You would have nothing to measure your achievements against; neither would you know where your efforts ultimately lead.

It would help if you had goals to ensure that you have direction in life. This direction would define your purpose in life, make your experience most interesting, and have you motivated in your work.

With a set goal, you will be able to decide better what job is best for you, what type of relationship you are looking for, what leisure habits you could pursue, and so on. Life is much better when you have a set goal because then you have something to set your compass for; you have a destination, and through it, you gain a direction.

Create To-Do Lists

The "To Do" list will tell you how many things you have to

do during the day, which is the no.1 priority and which can be deferred. It will also tell you how many tasks you have accomplished over the period and how many would need to be reinstated in tomorrow's "To Do" list.

Please make no mistake of writing off this tool as insignificant or trivial because it most definitely is not. The "to-do" list is perhaps the most critical of all time management tools; one that will keep your mind uncluttered and focused, motivated to complete tasks each day.

Each day completed tasks will build towards achieving the ultimate – your life's goal. The day is ultimately the smallest complete unit of your time and the "to do" list will ensure that it is used effectively and purposefully.

There is another huge benefit you will enjoy from using the "to do" list – and that is, you will be able to measure your progress. At the end of the day, when you see all those completed tasks scratched off the list, you will feel good about yourself and hugely satisfied that you have achieved so much. This feeling of satisfaction will act as a motivator to work more and better the next day, convinced and happy that you are moving in the right direction, and you are going to achieve your goal.

Do not work on tasks that are not present in your to-do list. When a new project or activity comes up, please include it in your "To-Do" list and assign its priority before working on it. If you will not add new activities in your list, and instead perform them as they arise, you won't be able to control your schedule. You might even waste your precious time on unimportant activities.

There are various time management systems that you can use today. You can download a time management app on your smartphone. You may install time management programs onto your computer. If you are "old school", you may use a pen and a notebook to plan your day. It doesn't matter which medium you will use, as long as you can view or edit its contents quickly and easily.

Making a Schedule and Sticking to It

Schedules can make life so much easier. You can use a

calendar, your phone, or even just a notebook. All of the most successful people keep a schedule. It is the single most critical thing you must have. Schedules can help you keep track of time and things that you have done and need to do.

When you have commitments, make sure that you write them into your schedule immediately. By doing this, you can see exactly where you have time for other things. Make sure that you think ahead when you are scheduling to give yourself time to get to different events or appointments. If you have appointments 20 minutes apart and it takes you 30 minutes to get to the second one, you don't have enough time.

Calendars are great because you can hang it on the wall or have it on your desk. So when someone calls or you have to make an appointment, all you have to do is look at it. It is also helpful if other people in your house have things to schedule as well. It is beneficial if you have to take them to these appointments or other events. It is something that you will have to look at every day, so it makes it harder for you to forget. It also makes it harder for others to schedule overlapping events.

Phones always have calendars on them. You can enter information into them to keep track of your schedule daily, weekly, or even monthly. You can also add alarms and reminders into the calendar to keep you on schedule. It can be one of the best tools when it comes to managing your time. This is especially helpful for people who take medication. You can set alarms to make sure that you take them on time and at the same time every day.

Computers also have calendars, it is great for someone who spends a lot of time on the computer for work. You can pull it up and see what you have planned.

Time Blocking

Blocking your time is one of the most effective ways to get tasks done. You use this strategy on complex tasks that require focus and many hours of work.

To start time blocking, you need to choose one task. You should then remove all the distractions around you before you start working on that task. If you have anything else scheduled in the next hour, you should reschedule it. It would be best if you also tell the people around you not to disturb you for the next hour. If this is not possible, you should relocate to a place where no one can bother you.

Before you start working on your task, you should declare your goal for this task. Your goal will determine if you are completed or not. In the next hour, you should work only on your chosen task. If it is not done yet by the time the hour ends, you should block another hour for the task. It would be best if you only stopped working when it is done or when you have more critical responsibilities in line. If you have to leave your current task without finishing it, you should find the next time slot for it before moving to a new activity.

The lack of focus can easily alter one's level of productivity. Instead of accomplishing tasks on time, you can waste hours procrastinating at your desk. An excellent strategy to help you manage your time better is called time blocking. The concept is pretty simple. To make every workday as productive as possible, you should assign specific tasks to specific time blocks during the day.

Hard as it may seem, scheduling tasks on fixed time blocks work quite effectively because doing so trains the mind to work with time limits per task. It is also a great way of keeping track of your work. By having distinct time allotments for your entire shift, you can do away with costly distractions and unproductive multitasking. Every minute has a purpose.

Although many people consider multitasking to be a particular skill, it has been proven to be counter-intuitive to being productive. It removes a distinct focus away from each of the tasks at hand. Instead of tasks being completed, each one is left partially done.

With time blocking, you can ensure that you achieve certain levels of progress on specific tasks at the right time. By having a full-proof structure in place, you get to experience close to double the productivity that you are used to given your standard workweek. You will be surprised as to the number of tasks you get to accomplish in a shift.

Like other time management strategies, to succeed at time blocking, you need to engage yourself in severe and dedicated planning. It is crucial that you give sufficient time for preparation. By doing so, you can save more time during your workweek for other, more meaningful, activities. Your time spent planning will indeed be time well spent.

You can do this overnight, before heading for the sheets, or in the morning as you prepare for your upcoming shift. Start by writing out about three to five of your most essential tasks for the day. Focus on tasks that need to be completed. Follow this list with another one this time carrying three to five secondary tasks, those that can be pushed to the next day if time doesn't permit their completion.

Always remember to divide the tasks accordingly. Be mindful of the time you allot for each one. Although it can be tempting to make a schedule that fits everything into the day, always remind yourself to be practical. The goal is to finish as much as you can without pushing yourself too hard. Keep in mind that if you become overwhelmed with your schedule, you may find it challenging to focus and end up procrastinating.

Start the Day Right

It would help if you began managing your time from the moment you wake up. If you wake up an hour earlier than everybody else does but you spend your first-hour reading emails, you are no different from the people who wake up an hour later but get directly to work. To start your day right, you need to become an early riser and be productive before everybody else.

Start early

You will have more time to work if you wake up early. If most people in your line of work wake up at 6 AM, you should wake up at 5 AM. It would help if you did this to avoid all the stresses that come with rush hour. By waking up an hour early, you will be on the road earlier than most people will. It will allow you to avoid traffic jams, you will arrive at your workplace and start on your tasks earlier than everybody else.

Make your bed
When we were young, we were instructed to make our beds the moment we got up. However, some of us never developed this habit. If you want to be successful in controlling your time, you need to do this symbolic activity. It symbolizes that you are starting your day the right way.

Sit down and plan your activities for the day
After making your bed, you should also take 30 minutes of each day to prepare. It would help if you started working on these tasks by including them in your schedule.

Planning should always follow the habit of making your bed. By doing it this way, it will be easier for you to make planning a practice. As mentioned above, your mind loves patterns in your actions. The more you do these two activities in the right order, the easier it will be for you to start your day.

Wake your mind with the right stimulation
After planning your day, you should choose an activity that will wake your mind up. Most people take a bath right after waking up as doing so sends a cold or warm sensation throughout the body. In a way, it wakes the senses up.

To maximize the effects of these activities, you should create a morning routine with them. Your morning routine is another habit that you can stack with the two mentioned above. You should include all the activities that will instantly wake your mind up from its low-energy state.

Focus on how you start your workday
Your success for the day usually depends on how you start it. When a person moves from one home to another, for example, he is generally confused with how to start his day. The things that he needs are not in their proper places—at least not just yet. The environment is new, and it takes the person a few moments to think before he can to start his routines. For people who cope poorly with changes, these small differences in the environment may affect their whole day. The bad start in the day also affects their attitude towards work.

Coming Up with Methods to Make Your Chores Easier

The most significant part of our society is that there are creative people who are continually coming up with new inventions to make lives more comfortable. Don't think of these inventions as an excuse to be lazy, but rather, look at them as an opportunity to get more accomplished faster. Not only are there great inventions to help you with your life, but you can also come up with hacks and other methods to make what must be done easier and less time-consuming.

Use Tools that Make the Job Easier

We may make fun of people for some of the ideas that they try to market, but some of the tools to make life easier. Try taking some of these tools and making them work for whatever you're working on at the time. If you're in charge of cooking a meal, try using the microwave tools that will help you to accomplish the same quality of the product without as much hassle. If you find that you do some tasks more often than others, find tasks that will help you to get them done faster with the same quality.

Learn Tricks to Getting Tasks Done from Others

People are always finding creative ways to get what you want to accomplish done faster. It can benefit you to take a look at some of these tips and try using them when you're trying to perform tasks of your own. Numerous websites offer advice and hacks on how to do everyday household tasks in different ways that you may not have thought about. Take some time and explore alternatives, it will help you out a lot especially if it is a task that you often do.

Look for Ways to Cut Corners Without Cutting Quality

You may think that cutting corners on a project can harm the quality of the result, but there are ways to do this without compromising the quality. Find ways to cut corners in everyday tasks so that you can get the job done faster. If you find that cutting corners cuts quality, find other ways to make the task easier.

Take the Advice of Others and Try it

The significant part about family and friends is that they have a wealth of tips and advice to make life easier. Don't be afraid to try some of this advice to make your own life more manageable. Some of it may work for you, while other bits of advice might be useless. The point is that you won't know if it's useful or not unless you give it a try!

Establishing Your Daily Activities

When planning your daily activities, you will need two notebooks. The first one is a planner that you will use to list down all your future activities. When an event is scheduled, you should place it immediately in your planner. You should carry this notebook around with you; thus, it needs to be compact and lightweight.

You should have this notebook with you every day to avoid putting your schedule in different tools. Some people have a planner in their computers, phones, and other devices. Because they shift from one medium to another when checking their schedule, the action never becomes a habit.

You should stick to only one planning tool. We suggest that you use a notebook planner because it is a one-function item. If you check your schedule in your smartphone, there is a good chance that you will be distracted by other notifications from your apps. This can distract you from the task that you need to do. On the other hand, a one-function tool allows you to schedule events with complete focus. When you are done checking your schedule, you will be able to go back to doing the next task in your list without distractions.

You will also need a second notebook that will serve as your time log. No matter how well we plan, we seldom follow the tasks that we set in our schedules. There are always unforeseen factors keeping us from doing things at the right time.

Prioritization

You cannot become an effective time manager until you plan what you need to do, prioritize your tasks, create a schedule, and give your work deadlines.

The key to proper time management is planning your work and giving tasks slots on your priority index so you can differentiate between urgent and non-urgent tasks.

When you draw up a "To-Do" list, the first thing you need to do is prioritize the tasks according to their importance and urgency. Importance and urgency are not the same – and rarely interchangeable though they seem so.

You need to prioritize the tasks according to your perception of urgency and importance. For example, answering the phone when it rings is urgent, but not always essential; meaning you can let the telephone ring sometimes when you are doing important work.

Be sure you understand which task is needed to be done first. There should be no doubt in your mind about what needed to be attended when this is why you make "To-Do" lists.

Once you put your mind to it, you will find it is relatively easy to decide which tasks you want/ need to be completed first. Do not stop until all your tasks are in a decisive order. Though you could always do it manually, this is where a little help from technology would be a significant boost in efficiency.

To ensure that you manage your time optimally, you need to break your main life goals into bite-sized sub-goals. In turn, these sub-goals may be broken down into tasks and action plans, so you know what to do, step by step to get there.

Prioritizing is also fundamentally important to effective time management. As we have seen, we tend to be more aware of what is urgent rather than what is essential. Prioritizing does not mean that you give importance to tasks. It means giving credence and letting the activities that count come first and leaving the other tasks for later. There are different approaches that you can use to prioritize what is essential and what is of lesser importance to you. There are two main ways that you can use to prioritize items on your to-do list:

Tackling the difficult tasks first
In this approach, you address the hardest tasks first before moving on to the more mundane tasks. The reasoning behind this is the same as the example of "eating the frog" that we had looked at in an earlier chapter. Tackling the harder and biggest tasks first is ideally meant to ease the anxiety and pressure that might necessarily hinder you from accomplishing anything.

Tackling easy tasks first
In approach number two, you first do the tasks that can be done in minutes and with minimal effort. One of the advantages of using this method is that once they are completed, you have less inconsequential tasks distracting you from achieving or completing the harder tasks.

You can combine the two methods by starting to making your "To-Do" list and then add priority stars to each time. The items that have the highest priority should get five stars while those with the least priority should have one star.

Make a list of all the tasks your project involves
Many people fail to recognize the importance of a taskmaster list. Plenty of people consider this to be a chore. What they don't realize is that spending a couple of minutes planning things out helps reduce the time spent completing a project by reducing the stresses and distractions that hinder a project's completion. It gives you the initial push, a clear direction, on how to begin your work.

Assess these tasks according to gravity and value
The thing about project management is that not all tasks are important. There are some which can be cut saving a lot of valuable time and effort. Look for the tasks that need the most attention, those which are of high importance to your output. Follow this by identifying which are of middle to low relevance. Always keep in mind that the more people have to be involved in a task, the higher its value usually is.

Organize these tasks into categories
Now that you have assessed each task for gravity and value, proceed with ordering. Arrange them based on the amount of effort required to accomplish a task. Also, provide an estimated time of completion for each one. It may be best

if you start working on tasks requiring the lengthiest amount of time to complete but, you can do the opposite if this suits your abilities better. Again, go with a process that works best for you and your team.

Determine which tasks to cut

As you move along and gain more knowledge of how to proper prioritization, you will see how effective and productive you can be in the workplace, given proper task scheduling and planning. Practice your skill with each project that comes your way and you will be a pro in handling your workplace demands, simple or complex.

Prepare Your Planning tools

To become a successful time manager, you need to have and use personal planning tools. These tools will help you plan, organize, and take control of your time. Some of the individual planning tools you will need are a calendar, pocket diary, wall charts, notebooks, computer programs, electronic planners.

If you are an auditory learner, you may prefer dictating your thoughts instead of writing down your tasks, activities, priorities, and schedule. It is OK; the important thing is finding a planning tool that works for you and a tool you can use consistently. When using a planning tool, always remember to:

Record every activity or event on your tool. If you write them down, it will be easier to allocate time to your daily tasks or activities. In addition, writing your activities down is the only sure to ensure you do not fail to plan for important activity.

Have your planning tool with you every time; for instance, carry your diary. Because you can refer to your planning tool, you will know which activity or task is up next.

Review your planning tool daily. It will help you measure your progress, determine how far you are from reaching your goals, as well as what more you need to do to achieve your goals.

Regularly Recharge the batteries in your electronic planner and synchronize it with your computer. This way, you will avoid unexpected power problem that will lead to unforeseen delays and time wastage.

Have a back-up system. A back-up system will come in handy when your original planning tool experiences problems; for instance, if you may lose or misplace your diary, or your computer may crush leading to the loss of your documents.

Get Organized

Disorganization leads to poor time management because it causes you to waste valuable time searching for an important tool or document from a pile of clutter. By looking at a cluttered work desk, you may feel as if you have much work to complete and may end up avoiding your work.

It is true that you can have goals, time plan, priority list, and schedule, but if you are not organized, accomplishing your goal may not be as easy. By organizing your working area (e. g study room, or office), you work efficiently without feeling overwhelmed.

An organized workspace can boost your productivity and save your time. If your workspace is clean, you can quickly find anything you need. You can also complete your tasks without going through mountains of unrelated stuff.

Time managers make sure that their workspace is clean. They ensure that each object on their table is related to the task they are currently working on. This way, they can prevent confusion and distraction. Thus, they complete their tasks quickly and efficiently.

Avoid Procrastination

Sometimes, you may want to put off some activities because they seem unpleasant or overwhelming. It will often leave much more undone, which keeps you from achieving your goal within the set deadlines.

To avoid procrastination, always engage in an activity when it is next on your "To-Do" list. Do not give yourself a reason or excuse why it can wait. To prevent procrastination, start the habit of doing activities or tasks now. To do that, you need to learn and remember the following things:

There is only now
Tomorrow is an unknown promise. The only time you have is now. What you do now will determine your future; if you decide to avoid an activity, you will be messing up your long goals because you will not accomplish your short-term goals. When you prevent an action today, tomorrow's "To-Do" list will be long, and you will end up feeling stressed.

Start doing your activity or task. By doing so, you will set your mind into action mode; you will let it know you have to do something. Slowly, the motion will gain momentum, and you will feel motivated to complete your tasks.

Once You Do It, You Will Be Ok
When you avoid activities and leave them undone, you feel stressed, and you have no peace of mind. To prevent this, try this method.

Pick an activity or task you have been procrastinating on for a long time. Start it now; you will realize the freedom that comes with doing an activity or task you have been avoiding. Make it a habit to do each activity on the scheduled time, and you will end up feeling good at the end of the day or week and at the same time, you will attain your goals.

Think About the Repercussions
If thinking about the benefits, rewards, or achievements that will come from completing a task or engaging in an activity does not work on you, and you find it hard to start on an activity, think about the adverse outcomes of not doing it. Think of the stress, nagging, lousy evaluation, and unattained goals that come with not completing a task or not engaging in an activity. Because you do not want this to happen, follow your plan, your schedule, and your day will be successful.

Do whatever it takes
Do anything that will help you complete a specific task. If it means locking yourself in a room or sacrificing some of your free time to achieve that task you have been avoiding, do it.

If it means writing it repeatedly every time you are scheduling your activities, write it. As stated earlier, you cannot write any activity for so many times and not come up with a solution for its completion. If you drop it from your list, you will tend to assume or forget it.

Take Breaks

At times, you may feel pressure when deadlines are looming and tend to work for more hours to complete your task or activity. I'm afraid this is not correct. Yes, you will complete your task before the deadline, but your productivity will be inferior because your mind will be tired and will not be able to focus on what you are doing.

Delegate Tasks or Activities

Start by identifying the tasks or activities that other people can complete and then select the appropriate person to achieve them. The relevant person will have the skills, interest, experience, and authority needed to accomplish the task.

When assigning tasks or activities, be as specific as possible, write down, and define the responsibilities, the deadline, and your expectations. However, give the person the freedom to personalize the task by letting him or her research, perform the task from a place of his or her choice, and perform it at the time of day when he or she is most productive and alert. It will help the person freely perform the task you assign them.

Occasionally, check on the person's progress and provide assistance where needed, being careful not to take over the responsibility. If the person was making good progress and did not request for assistance, leave the person be, and do not offer to help unless the person asks for help.

Reward the person for well-tackled activities or tasks; congratulate him or her and suggest improvements if needed. It will motivate the person, and the next time you will need him or her, he or she will be at your service because you recognize and appreciate their work.

You might be highly competent and, on most days, can handle every responsibility handed to you at work, but there are times when you will need extra sets of hands. It is where outsourcing and delegation enter the picture. It means having another individual complete a task on your behalf.

There is nothing wrong with delegating a task or two to someone else. Not only will it help meet deadlines faster, but it will also free up more of your time - time that can be used focusing on something more complex and in need of more considerable attention.

Delegation is an essential and highly beneficial time management strategy, and here are some simple steps that will help you overcome your doubts and trust your outsourced colleague.

Control your instincts to hard work

Everyone has an urge to be in control. In the workplace, there are plenty of professionals that are willing to take on more than they can handle because of this very reason. They put themselves in situations where they have to juggle multiple projects with coinciding deadlines.

You Can Delegate Down and What You Can Delegate Up

There is the task you can delegate up and the tasks which you can delegate down. Take a careful look at your "To-Do" list and identify which are the tasks that are mundane and routine; these could be down-delegated. Also, identify which of the tasks require special skills where others may be better skilled to deliver than you are; these tasks could up upward-delegated.

Give Clear and Concise Instructions

When you delegate ensure that you issue clear and concise instruction that leaves no scope for any type of ambiguity. To ensure that the instructions are clear, request that these may be repeated back to you. Often what you want to say, what comes out from your mouth and what is heard by the recipient can be totally different.

Build the Competence and Empower People for Down-Delegation

For a person to do an outstanding job, they need to own it. If they have to ask your permission or advice at every step, you might as well have done it yourself. Hence, the golden rule when you down delegate something is to give that person full authority and freedom for the completion of that particular task. In other words, the person should be able to do it his/ her way – not yours.

In order for them to do a good job, to your specifications, you need to ensure that their competency is built to the required level. Listen to what they need and encourage them to enhance their skills in every aspect they feel would improve their productivity.

Delegation Means "Let Go"

When you decide to delegate, it means you are taking that particular task off your plate. In other words, you would not pay attention to any of the details until it comes back to you completed. You may send a few reminders, just to keep things on track, but other than that you need to let go completely.

Avoid Multitasking

Many people are praising the benefits of multitasking. These individuals claim that they can perform different tasks simultaneously without sacrificing their effectiveness and efficiency. Unfortunately, studies have proved that this idea is completely untrue.

Before you can work on the first task again, you must perform another transfer of focus and energy. Here's an interesting fact: the "transfer process" itself is extremely tiring.

It is not unheard of that busy people proclaim how good they are at multitasking. Whether you are good at it or not is not the question.

The question is whether multitasking is a good tool for effective time management. The answer to this question is rather a two edged sword.

For some people, it is easy to perform two tasks at the same time while for others it is a bit difficult. What exactly is multitasking though?

Multitasking originated from the IT (information technology) industry. It is referred to as the parallel or interleaved implementation of two or more jobs. There are proponents of the skill that feel it is an essential life skill that helps one move fluidly between different tasks and work areas.

Plan Your Time

Plan for every second, minute, and hour of your day. Planning your time will depend on how you like to work, what time of the day you prefer to tackle given activities or tasks, and where you will feel more comfortable completing your task. To plan your day, you need to preplan your activities or tasks.

Some essential things you need to consider while preplanning your activities or tasks are:

Plan Your Day the Night Before

Before you go to sleep at night, make sure you have planned your activities or tasks for the next day. Write down your activities, starting with the most important ones; allocate each activity the time it requires, prepare all the resources you will need to complete each task and activity.

Do Not Get Overwhelmed

No matter how long your activity list is, or how busy your next day seems, do not feel overwhelmed. Instead, plan your day; plan how to tackle each task, schedule time for every activity, and remember the importance of, and rewards or benefits you will get from completing each activity on your list. At the end of the day or week, you will have accomplished your goals without complaining of how much work you had.

Wake up Early

Start your day early; although waking early may be tough, try. Set an alarm and set it every night. Waking up early allows time for you to prepare both mentally and physically.

When you wake up early, your mind will be ready for the day's activities and you will have time to complete your morning routine before you start your planned tasks or activities. Early morning rush will leave you confused, which will lead to a confusing and stressful day. Additionally, if you did not have time to plan your time and activities the night before, by waking up early, you can do it in the morning.

Sleep Early

Sometimes, sleeping early requires you to make some sacrifices such as giving up on your favorite TV show, the internet, or chatting with a friend at night. To make the time management process a success, make these sacrifices. How can you wake up early in the morning if you slept late? It is possible, but you will feel tired throughout the day.

Your body and mind need to relax and prepare for the next day's activities. By resting your body (enough rest), you will concentrate on your activities and the chances of you falling asleep during the day will minimize.

Setting Deadlines

While scheduling tasks, it is extremely important to set a very real deadline. To complete a task on time, you need to know its due date; setting a realistic period gives you sufficient time to work on the task. If a task ends on Saturday, place its deadline to Thursday and start early.

This way, you will get ample time to work on it and will have extra time to review the task so you can correct any mistake you made earlier. Moreover, this helps you get spare time to tackle all the interruptions bound to disturb you.

It is vital to start your tasks earlier than a few days before their deadline so you do not have to fret about meeting the deadline and you get additional time to understand the task and its requirements.

Once you create a plan for your tasks, get started on completing them. Frequently refer to the schedule and plan you have created and ask yourself whether you are abiding by the schedule; doing this helps you stay true to your plan and follow it.

Moreover, please make a point of printing your schedule and pasting it in your workplace and home.

This not only benefits you, but it also helps everyone around you, especially those involved in the tasks you have started. By printing out your schedule and placing it at strategic locations, those closest to you find out the crucial things you are doing and the work they are supposed to do.

Eliminate Distractions

Distractions come in many forms; some are good while some are loathsome. They are a hindrance to getting things done. Most times, when you are working at your desk, you might get email notifications that distract you from what you are doing. Although this is not bad, there is a cause of concern when you start longing for the distraction so that you can stop your task. Eliminating distractions will help you accomplish more in little time. Below are guidelines that you can use to eliminate distractions and ensure that you achieve more.

Train your brain to focus

This is a fundamental part of eliminating distraction. Even though you might use headphones or other means to block out external stimuli, your mind is still the most significant distraction there is. If your mind is jumping from one topic to the other on unrelated subjects than what you are aiming to accomplish, there is no way you can remain focused. Training your mind can be done by learning how to control it.

Break down huge tasks

It is easy to get distracted when the task seems too big and impossible. It might even cause you to procrastinate. Huge tasks become more natural to accomplish when they are broken down into easier smaller ones that when combined, ensure that the big task is complete. Research has also found that it is easier to get the motivation to accomplish smaller tasks than it is to get motivation for larger tasks.

Track your time expenditure

As indicated earlier, distractions come in many forms. To remove distractions in your daily routine, it is vital that you track how your time is spent. This will assist you to learn which tasks attract much of self-distraction. A handy tool that you can use is a time tracker app that can be installed on your smartphone.

Block all distracting websites and apps

One of the most common distractions is the web. When that email notification comes in, and you are tempted to check what it is, the possibility is that you will also be tempted to make a brief stopover on Facebook and make a few comments and before you know it, 30 minutes are gone.

Create a schedule

As we have seen throughout this book, a schedule is

essential in helping you manage time. It is also useful in limiting distractions. If you set a schedule, it indicates that you have every intention of following it, and it is harder for you to get distracted.

Manage Interruptions

While working on a task, you are bound to come across two significant challenges: experiencing interruptions and bothersome unnecessary tasks and issues. Minimizing different disruptions that crop up as you work on critical tasks is crucial to the success of those tasks. In order not to become distracted and lose focus on what you were doing; you need to keep interruptions at bay.

Realistically, you cannot control everything that tends to interrupt you while you are working since not everything is in your control. However, you can change how you tackle an interruption.

The truth is that interruptions are cleverly disguised multitasks. This could be email notifications or ringers and beeps. It is almost impossible to ignore an email if you get the notifications; it has something to do with how we are hardwired. You may want to use productivity apps like Self Control, to keep yourself focused on what is important.

Work When You Need to Work

It would help if you work when it is time for you to work. When you are in the office, start working as soon as possible. Do not engage in idle conversations, read a magazine, or watch cat videos online. There are things you need to do. It would be best if you will start doing those things immediately.

Minimize all of the Interruptions

It's impossible to prevent all forms of interruptions. Whenever you face a disruption, try to minimize its effects by going back to your work quickly. If someone calls you, for example, don't waste time with pleasantries.

Never beat around the bush. Doing so will lead to wasted minutes (or even hours). If you need to call someone, you must write down the things you want to talk about. This approach lets you cover all of the critical points of the conversation quickly. Your list will also serve as a useful guideline for your call. If the conversation heads to a topic you didn't write down, you may apologize and go back to the crucial issues or end the request (i.e. if you have covered all of the points you listed).

Ask Other People

Other people are wasting your time. However, you cannot deny the fact that you also are wasting their time. It would be great if you could ask them about the things you do that affect their schedule negatively. This kind of conversation often leads to a win-win situation for the parties involved. Your coworkers can specify the things that affect their productivity negatively. Meanwhile, you will gain more information about the interruptions present in your workplace. Once you know how you waste other people's time, you will have better chances of managing your own time successfully.

Chapter 4: How to Set Boundaries and Learn to Say No

Sometimes, a snap decision will require no response. Humans tend to follow an unspoken social contract that dictates that when someone asks you to do something, your answer will usually be in the affirmative regardless of what other tasks you must focus on.

Learning to say no is a useful tool to cut out the less important activities in your life and focus on the activities that are most important to you. It is also vital that you be aware of how to differentiate between important and urgent tasks. Learning to set boundaries and saying no is very important if you are to succeed in your time management endeavors.

In the example in the previous chapter, we had looked at a decision that had to be made between going out for a cocktail party with friends and spending preplanned time with family. Depending on what is more important to you (in this case, family); one of these decisions will require a no. Setting boundaries, on the other hand, will help you know when you cross them and help you not to cross them.

When we say yes but want to say is no, we spend hours, days and sometimes months regretting the "yes" decision and feeling much resentment while wondering why we said it. In most instances, saying no to a lot of us brings about feelings of shame and sometimes guilt. For example, when you say no to your children on a particular matter, you might feel guilty and as though you do not love them as much as they think you do or that you do not care. It is a perfectly natural response to 'no'.

Setting boundaries and learning to say no is about prioritizing and having the courage to love yourself and say no, even at the risk of disappointing others. The most important thing is not to base your worthiness on the approval of other people. Instead, always remember that it is impossible to please everyone, even Princess Diana couldn't!

Learning to say no is symbiotic to productivity. Let us look at an example. If you were working on your computer on a strict deadline and you get a chat request from a friend whom you have not communicated with for long, what would your option be? Let the chat go un-responded to until you are through with your work or cut in on your deadline time and chat with your friend?

A lot of us will opt for the later and compromise on our work. It brings confusion and unnecessary adrenalin rush because we have to cover for the time we lost as the deadline approaches. Saying no looks like a mammoth task but, it is not. We are all faced with different scenarios on a day-to-day basis. Learning to say no will help you filter out what is not important and give you enough time to deal with the critical aspects of your life, which will significantly influence your level of productivity.

On the other hand, we cannot say no to everything. Developing an active time management schedule and skill will help you prioritize and recognize the things or activities that require a no and those that require a yes. It will also help you create a strong will and inner strength. Even though saying no or setting boundaries is a bit of a task, there are some simple steps that you can take to ensure that you develop the skill of effective time management.

Create a mantra

When you are sure you are going to say yes to someone you really want to say no to, it helps a lot to have a mantra. A mantra does not have to be a chant; it can be anything. A mantra is just something that you can use to remind yourself of your inner strength.

A good practice is to have a ring, bracelet, or necklace that you can stroke when the desire to say yes overwhelms you. Another useful tool is to have an actual mantra. In this case, choose something that adds more power to your resolve; "I can say no" is a good one. Tailor the mantra to your difficulty to say no.

If you have a lot of difficulty saying no, choose a strong mantra that helps you choose discomfort over resentment.

Keep a journal

One of the things that we have looked at is how after saying yes, we walk around being resentful, especially when we fail to set boundaries. When you are feeling resentful, write this down and note all the times that you experience this. It can help you to recognize which situations make you feel the most resentment.

Practice

Saying no is something that develops over time, but like everything else, you have to practice. There are individuals in our lives that we cannot be able to say no to instantaneously. It helps to start small.

Setting boundaries will help you greatly in determining what is and what is not important and will help you achieve more in areas of your life that matter the most. Setting boundaries also requires that you set up a schedule that you can follow. A schedule should not be too restrictive and should afford you some flexibility.

Chapter 5: Improve Your Productivity by Identifying Your Personal Values

Because time management and life management are inseparable, improving your productivity starts with determining your values. Keep in mind that managing time properly is impossible if you don't know the things you value.

Excellent time management involves harmonizing a set of events that you consider as a top priority. If you think an activity is a low priority, you won't exert any effort to manage your time well in doing it.

Answer this simple question: "Why are you doing what you are doing?"

The Purpose and Meaning of Your Life
Everyone needs a purpose and meaning. People become sad and anxious if they feel that their activities are irrelevant to their values and beliefs. If you know the "why" behind your activities, you'll know the "when", "what", and "how" of improving your productivity.

Improving your time management skills is useless if you think that you are doing unimportant things. If you are good at doing things that are in contrast to what you value in life, you will just become more anxious and frustrated.

The Most Important Things in Your Life
After determining your life's purpose and meaning, you must identify the things you consider as extremely important. What are the things you would stand for regardless of the situation? What are the things you would never do?

Your day-to-day activities should match your own values. According to recent studies, poor time management results from the difference between a person's inner convictions and the things he/she needs to do.

Believe That You Are Special
Each person is unique in terms of values. No two people have the exact set of things they consider as important. Appraisals form an essential part of your identity. They rarely change as you grow old.

You must find your real values and manage your time so that you are working (and living) according to those values.

Perform Self-Analysis
The following questions will help you understand your values. Once you have determined those values, use them as the basis for preparing your schedule.

How would you describe yourself to a stranger?

"If an alien asks you to describe humans, what would you say?" – This question will help you understand your thoughts about humans in general. Do you consider humans as kind and loving creatures? Alternatively, you classify them as devious entities that cannot be trusted?

"How would you define life?" – With this question, you will discover your life philosophy.

"What is your ultimate goal?" – Your response to this question determines the goal that you should achieve for you to feel complete. This goal has the most significant influence on your entire life.

Some Apps for Productivity
Focus Booster

The Focus Booster makes use of the Pomodoro Technique based on the previous chapter. It works like a timer with more features, allowing you to manage your time in small bursts while avoiding potential distractions. The great thing about this app is that it records sessions and presents it in a detailed spreadsheet that allows you to analyze your time. Together with this, you can get suggestions on how to use your time better.

Rescue Time

Unfortunately, Rescue Time isn't free. On the plus side – it is an excellent app to have with more features to speak of. It is the perfect app for people who do most of their work online or through a computer, whether its PC, Linux, Mac, or Android. Rescue Time essentially tracks down your computer activity and presents you with a chart showing how much time was spent on websites.

Any-Do

A comprehensive app, "Any-Do" is ideal for people who often work with others in a group. It is because of the main perk of "Any-Do" is to share the list with other people who are working on the same project.

Other than that, "Any-Do" carries the most essential features of a typical time management app. It includes shopping lists, "To-Do" lists, notes, reminders, and events. You can also sync the app with other devices.

Toggl

Toggl works mainly as a time tracker. What you do is turn it on and off whenever you're doing a task and labels it for future use or reference. You can even organize time tags, and for those who get billed by the hour, you can use it to track billable time. It's currently one of the apps being used by those who work remotely. Timesheets may be sent, exported, printed, and reviewed.

To Do Calendar Planners

Electronic calendars are so much more efficient, allowing you to create a task list and have yourself reminded before the crucial moment. It is precisely what the app can do, including synching of data, prioritizing tasks, and even attaching Google Maps to your tasks.

Remember the Milk

An app to remember, Remember the Milk lets you organize and manage your time through several devices. It works in computers and mobile phones and may connect with your Twitter, Google calendar, and Gmail. You can also separate task lists depending on priority or if they're for home, work, or even school.

Time Doctor

Another one for the team, this app helps track your time, provides reminders, reporting tools, and integrates with other computer networks. It has the additional benefit of monitoring sessions through screenshots, therefore allowing you to find out whether your workers are working. Unfortunately, the app isn't free.

Google Calendar

Something free from Google, this Calendar presents a task list with an estimated time of starting and getting them done. You can add or remove tasks as you go. You can put in new tasks, set appointments, and block time for certain activities. The great thing about Google Calendar is that it's very pervasive so that you can put it in your phone, your tablet, and your laptop. If you happen to lose your gadget, you can always obtain your account from Google so there nothing is nothing lost.

Todoist

Another time management app that works for both single users and group work, the Todoist lets you arrange tasks, set deadlines, and have yourself reminded of anything that needs to be completed. It helps you keep track of urgent projects and collaborate with other people in your team. It's available in several languages and can be synched through all your gadgets.

Focus @ Will

This app uses the power of music and neuroscience in boosting productivity. The app essentially provides a continuous release of music that is proven to help with brain activity. It is meant to be used for those cerebral activities like paperwork or when you're trying to write a paper. For menial tasks like cleaning the house: however, it won't be as effective. It's NOT available for free, so you have to consider that.

Atracker

This personal time tracker lets you find out everything you do the whole day through a comprehensive reporting. You can customize the options for the tracker, add more tasks, and check the ones that have already been finished.

Evernote

Evernote is one of the more popular time management apps in the market today. You can use it to organize, synchronize, edit, and store your tasks so that you can access it anywhere. It functions mainly like a post-it note that you can view from any device.

If This Then That (IFTT)

Another unique time management product, it makes use of a basic logical precept wherein one action triggers you into doing another. It has the same principle used in the "Rhythm Routine" discussed in a previous Chapter. The app, however, uses the term 'recipe' and offers a host of preset and customizable recipes. For example, IF you're in the office, THEN you put your phone into silent mode. IF it's Friday, THEN you take your laundry to the cleaners. It also comes with a "To-Do" list that works with GPS and Maps. Hence, if you go to a certain spot and your "To-Do" list has something that is to be done there, it would alert you to that task.

Chapter 6: How to Manage Your Work Environment

The term "work environment" here covers both your home and workplace – and any other place where you plan to do any activity. It is an accepted fact that to work best, a conducive atmosphere is important. If you are not happy with your environment, it becomes challenging to focus on the task at hand – since you would be constantly distracted by various irritants.

It is, therefore, imperative that you create an atmosphere around you that promotes optimal output for you and all those who work with you. This covers your style of working, the equipment you use, the people you work with, and your motivation level.

Get Rid of Physical Clutter

Clutter is like a hidden monster, who gobbles up your energy. You will find that wherever there is clutter, productivity decreases considerably. You need to get rid of clutter from your environment as well as from your mind if you want to be able to do your best at any given time.

Here are a few top tips to ensure that your environment is clutter free and stays that way:

- Everything needs to have a place – this is one of the most critical rules whether you are an office or home (or traveling). Everything needs to have a place. On your desk create a flow order where papers come on the left and are sent onwards on the right. The table top should consist of only those items you need to work with during office hours. The rest go in drawers or any designated place.

- Extend the workplace vertically – lack of space is often the most common reason for desk-clutter. If you do not have enough space to put things away in their own place, think about expanding vertically. Different sized open cubicles on the wall behind or besides can instantly de-clutter your environment.

- Add hidden storage space – think of where you can insert a couple of drawers and do so. Your desk would become a versatile storage unit if raised a little and then equipped with partitions and/ or drawers. You can add a hidden cabinet in many places in the work station. Let your creativity flow – or call in an expert.

- Organize drawers – just having drawers is not enough. Ensure that the drawers are designed to keep everything in place as well. Use partitions inside the drawer to ensure that you can reach anything you want even without looking. It's incredible how much your productivity can improve when you have all the things you need in their place.

- Clear the computer desktop either daily or weekly – if you are a person who saves everything on the desktop you will, in no time have a vast mass of files cluttering your desktop. Besides making it difficult to trace stuff, the clutter would also tire your mind. Make it a habit to send all data to their respective folders and clear the desktop – either by the end of business or at the end of the week.

- Filing of documents must be done immediately – in offices where the paper flow is high and, it is imperative that filing should be done the same day, every day. About 30 percent of work time is generally wasted looking for documents in an office. Do not allow this time to drain.

- Keep what you need around you – forget about the items that "I might need some time". Keep only things, which you need around you. Send everything away that does not need to be used on a daily basis.

De-cluttering Your Mind

De-cluttering of the mind is as vital as de-cluttering of your work environment. How do you de-clutter your mind? Here are a few tips that will ensure that your mind stays free so you could totally focus and concentrate on the task you have on hand.

- **Write it down** – here your to-do list comes in handy. Write down everything you need to do each day. Complete your next day's to-do list before you retire for bed. In this way, you know what you have to do when you wake up in the morning.
- **Use a planner** – what needs to be done in a week, a month, and a year can be fixed and outlined in a yearly planner. Put the planner in a place where you can see it clearly and daily.
- **Use technology** – don't send yourself mental notes and feel overwhelmed by the necessity to remember so many things or worrying about forgetting anything important. Use your smartphone to remind you about tasks, keep track of time spent, announce meetings and deadlines, and so on. In this, your mind will stay free to focus on the work and nothing else.
- **Leave office things in the office** – make it a point to shut off your mind to office matters the moment you step out of the office. The same applies to house issues; leave all your home worries at home and do not allow it to overlap with things you have to do in the office. It takes a little practice, but it is possible. Program your phone not to ring between 8 PM and 9 AM. Also, do not open office email once you are out of the office.
- **Take time to de-stress your mind** – you need mental relaxation to release the stress that builds during working hours, especially if your job involves a high-stress environment. Find out means to relax your mind, such as 5-10 minutes' meditation,

Staying Motivated

Staying motivated is one of the most significant challenges

people face with work. Whether you refer to household chores or office work, finding the drive within you to get things done is often quite tricky. How do you do it? How do you manage to keep your motivation high so you could accomplish all that you set to do?

Reward a Good Job Done

One of the best motivators is a reward at the end of the task completed. Make a list of rewards you are eligible for at the end of each task on your to-do list. It could be a cup of coffee, a game on your smartphone, a 5-minute break on Facebook – whatever motivates you.

Take a Quick Break

Breaks are excellent boosters for productivity. Studies show that people who take a break at intervals of 90 to 120 minutes actually are more focused and work better. Put an alarm for 90 minutes and take a break to do something relaxing – grab a healthy snack or a cup of coffee, play a game, do a 10-minute meditation session, listen to a song, etc. Aim to keep the break under 15 minutes to enjoy the best results.

Watch Out for Time Killers

Perhaps one of the most significant challenges you will have to conquer is how to deal with time killers. The first thing to do is to identify which are the tasks that kill your time most. Once you have the list, you work out a plan to minimize the damage. Here are the top 7 most common time killers:

Checking Emails

Unless strictly necessary otherwise, turn off the email notification function on your smartphone and allow a specific time to read-and-answer email every day. It could be early morning, around noon, or at the end of the day. Have an automatic announcement that gives the sender a heads-up about the time you usually check your email.

Watching TV

Watching TV is relaxing for most people, but if you end up watching something beautiful on every channel available, you will have precious little time left for doing anything else.

Please make a list of the programs you want to see and check the time it takes to do so. If you are comfortable with the time you spend watching TV, it is okay; but if you find that TV takes away too much from your productive time, work out a better schedule. Also, stick to it.

Commuting

Commuting is one of the biggest time gobblers, but there is little you can do about it. Try using the commuting time to complete tasks that are time-consuming but do not require too much focus – such as checking your emails, sending memos, organizing your to-do list, researching for presentations, online shopping, **etc.** this way you are limiting the time wasted.

SmartPhones

It's lovely to have a phone that can do so many things – emails, games, online shopping, banking, etc. On the other hand, the smartphone can become an addictive time killer. Resist chatting/ talking on the phone more than you need. If your calls take longer than 2-3 minutes, you are doing it wrong. Communicate instead through chat apps – which allow you to reply in your time.

Resist the impulse to "just check the notification" for Facebook, Twitter, games, emails and so on. You would think you would just take a look, but then you would be tempted to play a game, answer another email, check out the offers and before you know half-an-hour has passed while you were on the smartphone.

Friendly Chatting

While it is important that you maintain a good rapport with your colleagues at work, it is best to keep chatting limited to coffee/ lunch breaks. Friendly chatting can steal up to 2-3 hours of your time every day. Discourage friends and family reaching you on the phone unless it is strictly necessary. Have the friendly phone chats over the weekends, while you commute to and from your work or in the evening.

Surfing the Net

Surfing the Net is one of the biggest gobblers of time. Whether you start by reading the headlines or watching a YouTube update, you will find spiraling into surfing for this and that and before you know it 1-2 hours have gone. Stay focused when you surf the Net; use it only for what you need for the task at hand.

Social Media Networks

Facebook, Twitter, Pinterest, and so on are addictive. You feel you will check it out for 2-3minutes and end up spending 2-3 hours over it. Allot time for this purpose so it would not interfere with your work schedule.

Chapter 7: Managing Time Spent with Other People

Regardless of how well you can manage your time, the people around you may not be as passionate about being efficient. It would help if you accepted now that you could never control how other people think and behave. You can only manage your interactions with them to minimize the chance of wasting time. Here are tips on how to avoid wasting time when there are other people involved:

Always have a goal when meeting people during work hours

You are sacrificing productive time when meeting during work hours. You are using the time that you could have spent working on important projects. It would help if you have a good reason for sacrificing such a valuable time slot.

To make sure that you do not waste the time meeting with people, you should have a goal coming into the meeting. The goal has two purposes: 1) it makes your behavior purposeful, and 2) it tells you when the meeting should end. If you do not have a goal coming into the meeting, the small talk may last too long. If you sense that this is happening, you should ask yourself if the intention of the meeting has been achieved. If so, you should end the meeting in a polite way.

Share information relevant to the meeting in advance

If you are expecting a meeting, you should tell people about the agenda of the meeting as well as the types of input expected of them ahead of time. This will arm people with knowledge coming into the meeting. When you ask the questions, they will be quick to answer you because they are prepared. It will reduce the time spent thinking of answers. You will also have a more productive meeting this way because your team will have more time to think of constructive ideas before the meeting. This will save the group a great deal of time.

Reduce chances of miscommunication

Miscommunication is one of the ultimate time wasters in a group setting. If there is miscommunication, group members may not be clear about what needs to be done. Their activities may not help achieve the group's goals.

Lead when no one wants to

A group should always have a leader. If no one wants to take the leadership position, you should take it. If you do not, all the group's meetings will be a waste of time. The efforts of each member will not be coordinated. Meetings will also become chaotic.

Most people do not want to take this position because they do not want to appear bossy to their friends or coworkers. t would help if you did not allow this fear from preventing you from controlling the use of your time.

Chapter 8: Health's Role in Time Management

Health is a critical factor in a person's well-being. You cannot function correctly unless you are relatively healthy both in mind and body. It is imperative that you develop and maintain a healthy lifestyle if you want to perfect the art of time management.

Eating right
Eating right is at the root of good health. Take a look at your eating habits and take steps to improve wherever there is scope. You need not go for any drastic measures; instead, you aim at adding better value to what you put on your plate.

- Increase the number of colorful vegetables (green, orange, red, purple, etc.) on your plate.
- Snack on raw vegetables and fresh fruits as much possible. When eating fruits pay attention to the sugar content if you have diabetes or have a family history of diabetes.
- Reduce the intake of processed and preserved foods.
- Change to grass-fed meat and wild-caught fish. Eat organic vegetables whenever possible.

- Eat 4-5 small meals instead of 3 significant meals.
- Moderate your intake of coffee and alcoholic drinks.
- Quit smoking.
- Carry nuts, carrots/ celery stick for quick snacks instead of junk food.
- Pack your lunch for a healthier (and pocket-friendly) meal.
- Drink plenty of water. Dehydration is a huge energy drainer.

Exercising

Exercising is of paramount importance today when the majority of physical-effort -intensive tasks are carried out by machines and computers. Your body needs to exercise not only to burn calories and keep weight in control but also to ensure that the muscles in the body stay fit and the systems within your body function optimally.

Don't worry, you need not enroll for heavy-duty gym workouts. Simple exercises can help. Here are a few simple steps that will keep you fit physically:

- Do a 10-minutes stretching routine first thing in the morning.
- Walk for 30-90minutes every day. It need not be even brisk walking. Just walk as you normally walk, but do it every day. To ensure best results, change your route and speed every week.
- Park your vehicle a little away from your workplace so you could benefit from the walk.
- Always take the stairs if there are 1-2 flights of stairs to navigate.
- Pace around when you are on the phone.
- Invest in a health monitor watch (it comes as low as $20). It will tell you when you need to get up from your desk and do some walking.
- Use the commercial break to do some quick exercises (choose your routine beforehand).

Sleep
Another crucial factor which contributes to your health is sleep. Busy people feel that it's okay to encroach in the time meant for sleeping to complete a task. Wrong. Stealing your sleeping time will tire your brain and lead to many severe problems such as impaired memory, inability to focus, decreased ability to solve problems, indecisiveness, and so on.

You need to sleep at least for 5-6 hours every night. If you must encroach in your sleep time, ensure that within 7 days you make up for the time lost by sleeping in a little extra. Pay attention the following must-dos:

- Night sleep cannot be replaced by day rest. The brain repairs and regenerates itself during the night sleep – not daytime sleep. It explains why people who work the graveyard shift feel tired and rundown in spite of sleeping almost the whole day to make up.
- It would help if you eat your last meal at least 3-4 hours before bedtime. Heavy and undigested meals interfere with the quality of your sleep.
- Ensure that there is no distraction (such as noise, light, too cold or too hot atmosphere) while you sleep. Keep the TV out of the bedroom if possible.
- Use an alarm to wake up so you would not worry about waking up on time – which will not allow you to sleep peacefully.
- Ensure that the bedrooms are adequately aired so you can breathe in fresh air while you sleep.
- Go to bed at least 2-3 hours before midnight. This part of sleep is the most beneficial for your brain function.
- Wake up the same time every day – even on holidays.
- Develop a habit of taking power-naps midday for a boost in brain function and energy.

Fun Time and relaxation
You cannot work best unless you have enough time to have fun as well. It would help if you balance your work hours with pleasure. Make time for hobbies, leisure activities

that give you joy and make you laugh.

Laughter is, indeed the best medicine. Hearty laughter removes the harmful effects of stress from your mind and body. You need to socialize with friends and feel loved and appreciated. It is imperative that you have fun and good times with someone who loves you. This is why pet therapy works so well with terminal patients and people who live alone.

Relaxation and fun are terms used interchangeably, but they aren't the same. While fun is relaxing, relaxation is time off to rest or do nothing. You may use your weekend to relax and have fun – as this would recharge your energy and renew your zest to work.

Chapter 9: Identifying Things That Waste Your Time

Time Killers

Time killers get the best of all of us at times. These are things that cause you to be late, not reach your goals, not be able to complete tasks or make you lose track of time. Of course, you want to get things done and if you have the drive and motivation, then you need to watch where your time goes. It can be any number of things. Below are examples of things you may be doing that are time killers.

- Spending too much time on Social Media. For example: Facebook, Twitter, Snapchat, Instagram, or even dating sites. You may want to check it r quickly to see what is going on, but then you find yourself watching videos or just scrolling for an hour. It happens to the best of us from time to time. However, if you are aware, you can stop this habit. Alternatively, make it part of your personal time.
- Procrastinating. (This is one of the biggest time killers. Putting things off because you think you can just do it later) If you keep putting off something because you don't like it, it will not be any better when you finally get around to doing it. It may make it worse because you have had so much time to think about it. Just do it and get it over with.
- Overbooking yourself. You can't be everywhere at once. You don't always have to feel obligated to do what

people ask of you. Always think about what you need to do first and make sure you have the time. You will have to accept the fact that people will always expect things from you and that it is okay to let them down sometimes.

- Watching too much TV. Give yourself a time limit. An hour a day is usually enough relaxing and unwind in front of the TV. And you can find small things to take care of during commercial breaks. You could sweep the kitchen, take the dog for a walk or even get in a little exercise.
- Spending too much time looking at your cellphone. (most people are guilty of this) A cellphone is a great device, but don't become a slave to it. If you can't go an hour without picking up your cell phone, then you are spending too much time on it.
- Worrying about things that you can't change or control. If you can not do anything to change a situation, then don't waste your time worrying about it. It will consume you and keep you from doing the things that need to be done.

There are many things that cause us to waste time. The things that waste our time are different for everyone, but the outcome is the same. We end up overworked and overstressed with nothing to show for it because we never finish the things that need to be done. When you tend not to get things done it causes you to stress out and waste even more time. It is a vicious cycle, but you have the power to stop it. Now is the time for you to take back your life and your time.

You can be productive and successful. The first step is identifying your time killers and start weeding them out.

Dealing with Time Wasters

When you are working on your important tasks, you should not allow other people or events to divert your attention from what you need to do. If you give notice to time wasters, you will not get anything done. Here are some strategies on how you should deal with time wasters:

List your time wasters

This is what happens when the phone rings or when it notifies us that we received an email. We habitually give attention to the source of the signal. The first step to stop these things from affecting your productivity is to be aware of them. You should go back to your time log and check when these habits happen. When you have identified the culprits, you should make a list of the habits that cause you to waste time.

Resist the urge to respond to distracting stimuli

You should do the same with other sources of distraction that tend to have the tendency to take your attention away from your work. Some of the common causes of distraction are the television, smartphone apps, and unproductive tabs on the computer. You should remove them from your work area if you want to focus on your task. If this is not possible, you should learn to resist reacting to their notification signals.

Remove social media apps

Among the most common sources of distractions, today are social media apps. They are in our phones and other mobile devices so we can carry them pretty much everywhere. If you notice that checking your social media accounts is taking too much of your time, you should remove these apps from your phone. These apps are designed to get your attention and to keep you hooked on them for long periods. You should remove them from any devices that you use for work.

Make your breaks boring

When mental and physical fatigue sets in because of work, most people feel that they need a reward. They seek activities that provide them with a psychological or material bonus. The problem is that most of the rewards we give ourselves are addictive. Over time, we develop a craving for the reward. There comes a point when we unknowingly overdo the rewarding part of the process.

Keep your environment tidy

A messy environment can also be a reason for wasting time. It is difficult to find things that we need if the surroundings are untidy. You will also have some difficulty in moving around because of the mess. When put together, these small factors can cause you to waste a lot of time.

When tidying up, you need to create a space where you can move freely. It would help if you practiced the same principle at work and at home. If there are too many things lying around, you should consider reorganizing your space or giving some things away.

Prepare activities for waiting and commuting

Most people also consider traveling as a waste of time. Traveling is a time waster only if you do not do anything while you wait. For example, if you drive to work, you can listen to an audiobook while driving. It will allow you to catch up on your readings while on the road. If you love reading, you could also put digital books in your phone for those times when you are made to wait, like at the bus stop or train station.

Chapter 10: Managing Your Productivity

Divide your day into quadrants

During planning, you should divide your day into 4 quadrants. If you are awake for 16 hours per day, each quadrant should contain four hours. By planning your day this way, you will be able to put tasks into blocks of time. You will also be aware of how productive you have been by checking your output at the end of each quadrant.

We usually spend the first quadrant preparing for the day ahead; this is where your morning ritual takes place. If you live far from your workplace, part of this time will also be used for commuting. Part of this quadrant will also be spent for the start of your workday. You should take on your most essential tasks in this quadrant.

The second and the third quadrants are where the rest of the workday happens. It is when we are most awake and productive. The last quadrant is usually spent with the family over dinner (or personal leisure time if you live alone). If you have a unique project, you may also use this part of your day to work on that.

Divide each quadrant into 15-minute chunks

If the 4-hour quadrants do not work for you, you may also choose to divide your working period into 15-minute chunks.

A 15-minute period is long enough for you to start something and short enough for you to start and finish most of your shorter activities. Let's say you plan to work for an hour. You set your alarm to go off every 15 minutes. Every time the alarm goes off, you check your mood. If you still feel like working, you should continue until the alarm clock goes off again.

If you feel like you are tired when the alarm clock goes off, you should take a break. Your break time should only be 15 minutes long. The next time the alarm sounds, you should get back to work. It works better for people who get bored quickly.

This method is also beneficial if you often neglect essential tasks because you think there is not enough time. We often neglect tasks that we classify as "important but not urgent."

Manage your energy
Your will power to work weakens as your energy level goes down. By the time you start your final quadrant, your energy level is at its lowest. This is the reason why most people no longer have the will power to work at home.

Now that you know how your energy level depletes during the day, you should try to readjust your schedule so that the most critical tasks are done at the time of day when your mind is most awake. If you are working on a personal project outside of work, for example, you should put it in your schedule early in the morning right after your morning routine. If there is too much commotion at home, you can also do your project in your office right before you start the workday.

Motivate yourself for work right before a new quadrant starts
The advantage of dividing your day into parts is that you get to restart your day for each division. Let's say you are already tired after your day's second quadrant. Most people will give up on the workday. They will spend the rest of the workday with half the energy level they had in the morning. When doing their tasks, their attention is on time rather than

on their tasks.

It is not that they do not have the energy; they lack the motivation to do their work. Over time, this becomes a habit. They habitually decrease their energy level on the third quadrant of their day. For most people, the pattern develops because they forget their reason for working at this point of their day. Even if they were extremely productive in the morning, they still end up providing the output of mediocre quality.

If you usually enter the same mental state in the later parts of your day, you should find ways to re-motivate yourself right before you start a new quadrant. By doing so, you remind yourself of the things that motivate you to work.

Chapter 11: Improving Your Time Management Habits

Identify the nature of your activities
From your records, you should categorize your activities. For a working mother, for example, the activities may be divided into these categories:
- Family
- Work
- Personal time
- Socialization

Some of us are guilty of spending too much time in one category. We usually over-do something that feels good. The goal of categorizing your tasks is to become aware of how you balance your time. When you are aware that you are spending too much time in one aspect of your life, you will be able to modify your behavior.

Analyze and re-strategize
In this activity, you should examine your weekly planning notebooks. It would help if you compared your plans to what happened. If things did not go as planned, you should not be too hard on yourself. Instead of blaming yourself or others, you should focus on what you can do to prevent deviations from the plan in the future.

It would help if you looked for time-wasting events that

occur regularly. You should identify the causes of these time management problems and try to look for solutions. If a particular strategy does not work for you, you should look for other ways to deal with your time management problems. After all, dealing with the same issue may not always require you to stick to just one approach.

Look for positive changes and make them your habits

As you examine your logbook and your planner, you should look for areas where you have improved. You should see if there are changes that you can make that would further enhance your performance. It would help if you also made habits out of these positive changes. By developing time-conserving habits, you will be able to make positive changes permanent.

Aim for efficiency

The ultimate goal is to continually look for strategies that will improve your efficiency at work and home. You will only reach maximum effectiveness if you are no longer distracted by time wasters. You will need the self-discipline to resist the urge to give these time wasters your attention. However, if you successfully ignore these distractions, you will reach your goals sooner, and you will have more time for your other priorities in life.

Eventually, you will begin to improve your efficiency with time. As you improve, however, you may become complacent. When this happens, you will become more susceptible to distractions. You should continue applying the strategies suggested in this book so that you will never become complacent with how you use your time. It would be best if you also were alert for ways on how you can further improve your efficiency and productivity. If you feel like you are losing focus, you should reread this book again to remind yourself of what you need to do.

Chapter 12: Enjoying a Motivated and Productive Life

Enjoying life isn't necessarily about having free time and being great at everything. It's about disciplining yourself and making it a point to improve on your weak points. Some people are content with the way they are.

To enjoy your life as being motivated and productive, you must learn to put the procrastination habit on the shelf and leave it there to rot. It's not easy. If you are used to putting aside tasks until you feel like doing them, making yourself do them right away is going to feel uncomfortable for a while. Once you get into the habit, you will find that you enjoy being productive and laugh at yourself for the times when you would procrastinate it.

Not only will you enjoy being productive and managing your time well, but others will notice the difference in you. You will find that you're more relaxed and not feel pressured by large amounts of work. It will all come in time. You're not going to be able to change years of habits overnight.

Just remember, procrastination leads to stress, and stress leads to a less enjoyable life. Just because you're intimidated by the list of tasks before you, don't make the situation worse by procrastinating them. Take some of the tips that I've mentioned and make yourself face your struggle head-on.

Once you've found a balance between time management

and focus, you will notice that your tendency to procrastinate has gone way down. Great job! Continue to build healthy time management habits so that you won't fall into the trap of procrastination again.

There are a thousand and one ways that each of us starts our morning. Although some of us start our morning much later, all of us have a specific time that we consider morning. Productivity is usually very high in the mornings; hence, it is vital that you accomplish as much as possible during this time. It makes a morning routine a very fundamental part of effective time management as well as productivity.

Mornings are the perfect time to be creative, exercise as well as have some 'me time'. Additionally, science has indicated that a person's willpower is most influential in the morning. It means that if we want to be productive, we must take advantage of these and perform tasks that will be more difficult as the hour's pass. How you spend your morning is also a precursor to how your day shall progress. A calm and productive morning will yield calmness and productivity throughout the day, while a hectic and frantic morning ritual will generate much of discord during the day.

Conclusion

Thank you for making it to the end of this book. We all struggle with something in our lives. Time management is nothing but a plan to get the most out of your day and life. Contrary to common belief, it is not difficult to incorporate into your life – especially, if you have defined your life's goal. The moment you have your eyes on your goal, motivation to get your life in order will come to you automatically.

Remember, it's your life, and you can be as busy and as free as you want to be. Time management is just the right tool to hand over control of your life to ***you!***

It will also go a long way into helping you achieve your life goals as well as be in better control of your life and your time. If you implement all the skills that we have discussed, you will never have to rush at the last minute to get to your meeting or have a hectic unplanned morning. Your life will be seamless.

Tomorrow is a new day, make it your day for taking control and managing your time with precision and accuracy.

Try some of the tips and ideas in this book to help you to alleviate your procrastination manage your time and be more productive. It might be difficult at first to get yourself going, but once you do, you can be a force that will mean significant changes in your life and those around you! By recognizing that it is a problem, you're on your way to correcting it and becoming a better you!

www.ingramcontent.com/pod-product-compliance
Lightning Source LLC
Chambersburg PA
CBHW030018190526
45157CB00016B/3117